W9-BYH-412

Counting in the Rain Forest

Fredrick L. McKissack, Jr. and Lisa Beringer McKissack

Enslow Elementary
an imprint of
Enslow Publishers, Inc.
40 Industrial Road
Box 398
Berkeley Heights, NJ 07922
USA
http://www.enslow.com

To Mark, with much love.

Enslow Elementary, an imprint of Enslow Publishers, Inc.

Enslow Elementary® is a registered trademark of Enslow Publishers, Inc.

Library of Congress Cataloging-in-Publication Data

McKissack, Fredrick, Jr.
    Counting in the rain forest / Fredrick L. McKissack, Jr. and Lisa Beringer McKissack.
      p. cm. — (Counting in the biomes)
    Summary: "Children can count from one to ten as they read about the different animals, plants, and features of the tropical rain forest"—Provided by publisher.
    Includes bibliographical references and index.
    ISBN-13: 978-0-7660-2992-7
    ISBN-10: 0-7660-2992-1
    1. Counting—Juvenile literature. 2. Rain forest animals—Juvenile literature. 3. Rain forest ecology—Juvenile literature. 4. Rain forests—Juvenile literature. 5. Biotic communities—Juvenile literature. I. McKissack, Lisa Beringer. II. Title.
    QA113.M39656 2008
    578.734—dc22   2007020291

Printed in the United States of America

10 9 8 7 6 5 4 3 2 1

To Our Readers: We have done our best to make sure all Internet Addresses in this book were active and appropriate when we went to press. However, the author and the publisher have no control over and assume no liability for the material available on those Internet sites or on other Web sites they may link to. Any comments or suggestions can be sent by e-mail to comments@enslow.com or to the address on the back cover.

♻ Enslow Publishers, Inc., is committed to printing our books on recycled paper. The paper in every book contains 10% to 30% post-consumer waste (PCW). The cover board on the outside of each book contains 100% PCW. Our goal is to do our part to help young people and the environment too!

Every effort has been made to locate all copyright holders of material used in this book. If any errors or omissions have occurred, corrections will be made in future editions of this book.

Illustration Credits: Rick and Nora Bowers/Visuals Unlimited, pp. 3 (lorikeet), 18–19, 29 (lorikeet); Gregory G. Dimijian/Photo Researchers, Inc., p. 9 (top); Enslow Publishers, Inc., p. 4 (map); Dan Guravich/Photo Researchers, Inc., pp. 10–11, 28 (sloth); Jacques Jangoux/Photo Researchers, Inc., pp. 23 (big inset), 29 (lily pads); © 2007 JupiterImages, pp. 3 (chameleon, waterfalls, orangutan), 5 (inset), 9 (bottom), 14–15, 27 (left), 28 (chameleon), 28 (orangutan), 30 (chameleon); KUBACSI/Photo Researchers, Inc., pp. 21, 29 (bananas); Craig K. Lorenz/Photo Researchers, Inc., pp. 6–7, 28 (frog); Ken Lucas/Visuals Unlimited, pp. 3 (Komodo dragon), 25, 29 (Komodo dragon); © Marie Read/Animals Animals-Earth Scenes, p. 13; Shutterstock, pp. 1, 2, 3 (background), 3 (kookaburra), 3 (lily flower), 4–5 (background), 8–9 (background), 12–13 (background), 12 (inset), 16–17 (background), 20–21 (background), 22–23 (background), 23 (little inset), 24–25 (background), 26–27 (background), 26 (inset), 27 (right), 28-29 (background), 28 (kookaburras), 30–32 (background); Stuart Wilson/Photo Researchers, Inc., pp. 17, 29 (orchids).

Cover Illustration: Gregory G. Dimijian/Photo Researchers, Inc.

Contents

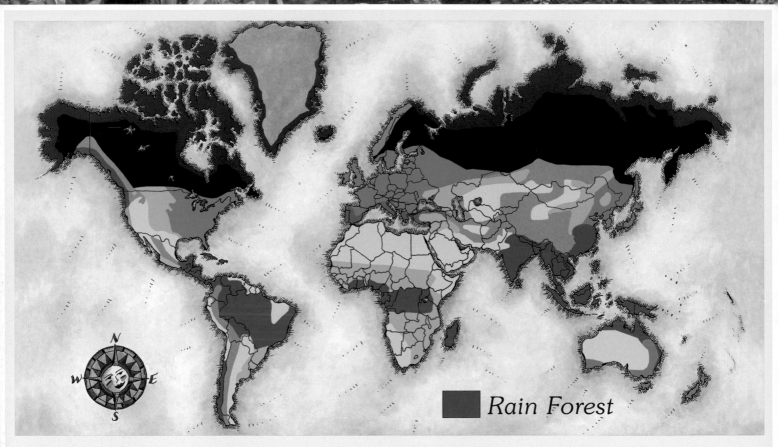

Rain Forest

What is a biome? A biome is an area of land or water with special plants and animals that need each other to live. There are many different kinds of biomes. Each biome has different kinds of weather.

In this book you will find out all about a place called the rain forest.

rain forest—There are two types of rain forests:

1. **temperate (TEM-per-it) rain forest**—Most temperate rain forests are found near oceans. They get lots of rain and can be cold. Trees grow tall and close together.

2. **tropical rain forest**—Tropical rain forests are found near the equator (ee-KWAY-tur). The equator is around the middle of the earth. Tropical rain forests get lots of rain and are hot. Trees grow tall and close together.

layers of the tropical rain forest—There are four layers in a tropical rain forest:

1. **emergent (eh-MER-gent)**—Trees in the emergent layer are very tall. These trees grow above all the other trees.

2. **canopy (CAN-oh-pea)**—Canopy trees make a roof over the rain forest.

3. **understory**—Trees in the understory are short. They do not get as much sun as the canopy and emergent layer trees.

4. **floor**—Small plants with big leaves grow on the rain forest floor. Sunlight has a hard time getting all the way to the rain forest floor. The big leaves help plants get enough sunlight to live.

How many poison dart frogs do you see?

One

This **one** poison (POY-zuhn) dart frog lives in the rain forest. Poison dart frogs are small and come in many bright colors. These bright colors warn animals that may want to eat the frogs. If an animal licks the frogs' skin, the animal will get very sick.

Poison dart frogs eat bugs, ants, small beetles, and spiders.

How many eyes does a chameleon have?

Two

The chameleon (kuh-MEE-lee-uhn) has **two** special eyes. Its eyes can turn in different directions. It can look to the front and the back at the same time! The chameleon can also look out for other animals that may want to eat it.

Chameleons have another way to stay safe in the rain forest. They can change colors to help them hide in the trees. They can become green, yellow, red, black, or brown. Chameleons can even make their skin look like they have spots.

How many **claws** does a three-toed sloth have on each **foot**?

Three

The three-toed sloth has **three** long claws on each foot. It uses its long claws to climb trees in the rain forest. The sloth lives almost its whole life in the trees. The sloth sleeps all day and is awake at night. The three-toed sloth likes to hang upside down. During the night, it eats the leaves of rain forest trees.

The three-toed sloth is the slowest mammal on earth. It sleeps between fifteen and twenty hours a day.

How many **colors** is the male **kookaburra**?

Four

The laughing kookaburra (KOOK-ah-buhr-uh) is a bird that lives high in the rain forest trees. Male kookaburras have **four** colors. They have white, light brown, dark brown, and blue-green feathers. Female kookaburras do not have blue-green feathers.

The laughing kookaburra is known for its bird call. The call sounds like a laugh. It says "kook-kook-kook-ka-ka-ka."

How many **fingers** does the **orangutan** have on each **hand?**

Five

The orangutan (oh-RANG-u-tan) has **five** fingers on each hand. The fingers help it swing from tree to tree in the rain forest. Orangutans are one of the few animals that live most of their lives in trees. They are the biggest animals to live in trees. Every night they build a different nest in a new tree.

Orangutans are part of the ape family. Apes are mammals that have long arms and legs, hair, and no tails. They are very smart. Most apes live in groups. Orangutans are different from other apes because they like to live alone.

15

How many **orchids** do you **see**?

Six

These **six** orchids (OR-kids) grow in the rain forest. Orchids need lots of water to grow. The rain forest is a great place to find orchids. Orchids can grow on the ground or high up in rain forest trees. When they grow in trees, they wrap their roots around the tree.

1

How many colors is the rainbow lorikeet?

Seven

The rainbow lorikeet (LAWR-uh-keet) is a colorful bird. It has **seven** different colors: blue, orange, purple, red, gray, yellow, and green. The rain forest is full of many bright colors. The lorikeet can hide among the different plants and flowers of the rain forest. They live high in trees and do not land on the rain forest ground.

Lorikeets live in big groups called flocks. A flock can have as many as twenty lorikeets or even hundreds! The birds fly, live, and hunt for food as a group.

19

How many **rows of bananas** do you **see** on this **banana tree**?

Eight

Many foods that we eat come from the rain forest. Bananas grow on large plants. About **eight** rows of bananas will start growing on one plant. The leaves of the banana plant open to show the fruit inside. People all over the world eat bananas. Animals eat them too.

Banana farms are part of the rain forest. This means that farmers do not need to cut down the rain forest to grow banana plants.

How many giant water lilies do you see?

Nine

These **nine** giant water lilies float on rivers and lakes in the rain forest. The giant water lily is a plant with one very big leaf. Fish and animals eat the giant water lily for food.

This big leaf starts from a small seed the size of a pea. Giant water lilies can get so big that you could lie on it like a bed. The giant water lily is also very strong. It can hold more than one hundred pounds without sinking.

How many **claws** does the **Komodo dragon** have on its **front feet**?

Ten

The Komodo (kuh-MOW-doh) dragon is the biggest lizard in the world. It has a total of **ten** claws on its two front feet. Most lizards eat insects and plants. Komodo dragons eat meat. They use their claws to hunt and kill other animals.

Young Komodo dragons live mostly in trees, eating birds, eggs, bugs, snakes, and other animals. Adult Komodo dragons hunt for food on land. They will hunt deer, pigs, and even buffalo!

More Information on the Rain Forest

Rain forests are found all over the world. Most are near the equator. The equator is an imaginary line around the middle of the earth. Rain forests are very wet biomes. They get a lot of rain every year. Water drips from tall trees and rivers flow through the land.

Tropical rain forests are also very hot. Hot and wet weather makes the air humid. Humid air feels heavy and wet.

Many different plants and trees grow in rain forests. Some trees are very tall. Some plants are so small they grow along the ground. Because there are so many trees, sunlight has a hard time reaching the ground.

There are a lot of different animals in the tropical rain forest. Over half of all the animals in the world live there. Snakes, birds, fish, bats, monkeys, tigers, and

even some elephants live in the rain forest. Some animals live on the forest floor. Others live high in the trees. Some animals spend almost their entire lives living in the trees. These animals rarely touch the ground.

Animals in the rain forest eat plants and other animals for food. The pitcher plant is a plant that eats animals! When small animals and bugs try to drink the sweet nectar around the rim of the flower, the plant traps them and eats them.

People sometimes cut down parts of the rain forest to clear the land for farming. It is important to take care of the rain forest. People all over the world need tropical rain forests. Many rain forest plants are used to make medicine or food. Many fruits and

vegetables grow in the rain forest. Plants and trees also help make air for all of us to breathe.

Count Again!

1		**One**
2		**Two**
3		**Three**
4		**Four**
5		**Five**

Count Again!

6		Six
7		Seven
8		Eight
9		Nine
10		Ten

Words to Know

claws—A sharp fingernail on an animal.

flock—A group of birds that live together.

humid (HYOO-mid)—Air that feels wet.

layer—Different parts of something.

mammal—A warm-blooded animal that feeds its young milk.

tropical (TROP-i-kuhl)—Weather that is always hot and humid.

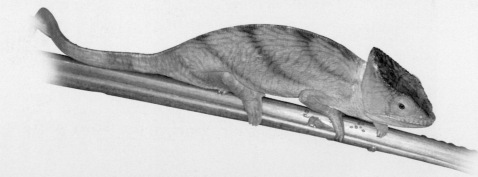

Learn More

Books

Doering, Amanda. *A Rain Forest ABC: An Alphabet Book.* Mankato, Minn.: A+ Books, 2005.

Flatt, Lizann. *The Nature Treasury: A First Look at the Natural World.* Toronto, Canada: Maple Tree Press, 2005.

Trumbauer, Lisa. *Discover the Rain Forest.* Bloomington, Minn.: Red Brick Learning, 2006.

Internet Addresses

Virtual World: Rain Forest at Night
<http://www.nationalgeographic.com/earthpulse/rainforest/index_flash.html>

Rain Forest
<http://www.mbgnet.net/sets/rforest/index.htm>

Index

A
animals, 4, 6, 8, 14, 22, 24, 26, 27

B
banana, 20
biome, 4, 26
bird, 12, 18

C
canopy, 5
chameleon, 8, 9
claws, 10, 24

E
emergent, 5
equator, 5, 26
eyes, 8

F
feathers, 12
fingers, 14

floor, 5
flower, 16
foot, 10

G
giant water lily, 22

H
humid, 26

K
Komodo dragon, 24
kookaburra, 12

L
layer, 5
leaf, 22
leaves, 5, 20
lizard, 24

O
orangutan, 14
orchids, 16

P
plants, 27
poison dart frog, 6

R
rain, 5, 26
rainbow lorikeet, 18
roots, 16

S
sunlight, 5, 26

T
temperate rain forest, 5
three-toed sloth, 10
trees, 5, 10, 12, 14, 16, 18, 20, 24, 26, 27
tropical rain forest, 5, 26

U
understory, 5